SELENA GOMEZ

Jenny Vaughan

LONDON•SYDNEY

First published in 2012 by
Franklin Watts
338 Euston Road
London NW1 3BH

Franklin Watts Australia
Level 17/207 Kent Street
Sydney NSW 2000

Series editor: Adrian Cole
Art direction: Peter Scoulding
Design: Simon Borrough
Picture research: Diana Morris

Acknowledgements:
Peter Brooker/Rex Features: 13.
© W. Disney/Everett Collection/Rex Features: 4, 10, 11, 15.
Helga Estab/Shutterstock: front cover, 18, 22, 26.
Everett Collection/Rex Features: 8.
JSS Images/BEI/Rex Features: 27.
Lisa Lake/WireImage/Getty Images: 21b.
MBB Images/BEI/Rex Features: 20.
Picture Perfect/Rex Features: 23.
Christopher Polk/Getty Images: 17b.
Soul Brother/Film Magic/Getty Images: 24.
Startracks Photo/Rex Features: 5, 7, 9, 16, 17t, 19, 21t, 25.
© Warner Bros/Everett Collection/Rex Features: 14, 29.

Every attempt has been made to clear copyright. Should there be any inadvertent
omission please apply to the publisher for rectification.

A CIP catalogue record for this book
is available from the British Library.

Dewey Classification: 791.4'5'028'092

ISBN: 978 1 4451 0657 1

Printed in China

Franklin Watts is a division of Hachette
Children's Books, an Hachette UK company.
www.hachette.co.uk

Contents

Words highlighted in the text can be found in the glossary.

Selena's a wizard

Selena's big breakthrough came in 2007. Aged 15, she got the part of Alex Russo in *Wizards of Waverly Place*. She played the only girl in a family where all three children were wizards.

Wizards was made for the Disney Channel. It had over 4 million viewers in the US alone by the time the last episode was made, in 2010.

This is Selena on the set of *Wizards of Waverly Place* from **season** one in 2007.

4

Wizards made Selena a household name – but, after four seasons, it ended. Now Selena is busy acting in movies and is the lead singer of her band, The Scene.

Selena made her first album, *Kiss & Tell*, with The Scene in 2009. It sold over 500,000 copies, giving Selena a **gold record**. The song "Naturally" from the album had over 1 million downloads.

"I basically want to make music that is fun and that parents and kids can jump around to and have a good time to."

Selena on her 18th birthday, with a gold record celebrating sales of 500,000 copies of *Kiss & Tell*.

Who is Selena?

Selena Marie Gomez was born on 22 July 1992 – her star sign is Cancer. She spent the first years of her life in Grand Prairie, Texas, USA. Her mother, Mandy, is half Italian, and her father is Mexican-American. Selena's parents divorced when she was very young.

Selena wanted to be an actress from an early age – following in her mother's footsteps. Also, her parents named her after a singer-songwriter, Selena Quintanilla-Pérez – so maybe she was destined to sing as well. Selena says her **role model** is "first and foremost, my mom".

Life was tough in the early years. "We lived from paycheck to paycheck," says her mother. Things have changed – Selena was paid around $25,000 for each episode of *Wizards*, making her the third highest paid teen star of 2010.

6

Selena with her mother, Mandy Teefey, in 2008.

> **"My mom did a lot of theatre... When she got ready for the show ... I would sit behind ... One day I said, 'I want to be like you!'"**

Early days

Selena was seven when she got the part of Gianna in *Barney and Friends*. The show featured a purple dinosaur, and was aimed at young children. It involved lots of singing and dancing.

Selena appeared on *Barney* for two years during seasons 7 and 8. Then the **producers** "felt like I was getting too old, so I got the boot".

Selena (sitting on the yellow ball) played the part of Gianna.

"I learned everything from that show ... A lot of people would be embarrassed to say they were on *Barney* but I embrace the fact and I had such a wonderful time ..."

Selena met her friend, Demi Lovato, on *Barney*. When she left, "I cried my eyes out because I thought I wasn't going to see Demi as much. Our parents decided to home-school us together."

It wasn't all fun though. She was picked on at school – "Because when you're in fourth grade, it's not cool to be on *Barney*."

Selena meets up with friend Demi in 2007.

Going  west

In 2005, the Disney Channel made Selena a guest star in *The Suite Life of Zack & Cody*. The next year, she played Mikayla, Hannah's rival, in *Hannah Montana.*

Selena starred alongside Miley Cyrus (centre) in *Hannah Montana.*

Then in 2007, Selena and her mother moved to Los Angeles. That was when Disney picked her to play Alex Russo in their series *Wizards of Waverly Place*. The show **premiered** in October 2007 and had nearly 6 million viewers for the first episode. Selena was on the road to fame. She was still only 14.

Moving to LA, "was hard ... It was almost a test of how badly I really wanted to pursue acting. Which I did, there was no question in my mind ... But it was really tough to leave my friends behind."

Wizards of Waverly Place soon brought Selena new friends. This is what she said about the other **cast** members of *Wizards*, also in 2007: "They basically ARE my brothers; they're my real family. My mom laughs at me ... because we're constantly in touch with one another ... I don't have any real life siblings so this way I can have brothers."

Selena, alongside her on-screen brothers Max and Justin in 2007.

Wizards

In *Wizards of Waverly Place*, all three Russo children had magical powers – but only the best one would remain a wizard after the age of 18. That made for plenty of rivalry in the family!

A made-for-TV film, *Wizards of Waverly Place, The Movie* was first shown in 2009. It had 11.5 million viewers. It was the second-most watched Disney TV movie ever – after *High School Musical 2*.

The *Wizards* website (see page 30) has pictures and interactive games, as well as news about the show.

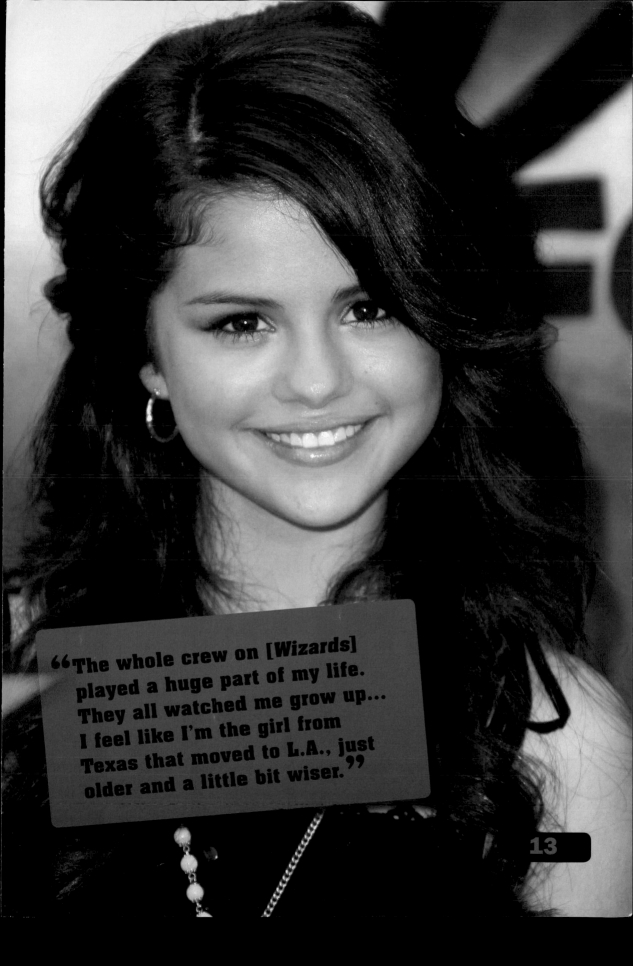

"The whole crew on [Wizards] played a huge part of my life. They all watched me grow up... I feel like I'm the girl from Texas that moved to L.A., just older and a little bit wiser."

13

Movie star

Selena's movie breakthrough came in 2008, when she got the starring role in a Warner Brothers made-for-DVD comedy, *Another Cinderella Story*.

In 2009, she starred in the Disney Channel original movie, *Princess Protection Program*. She played an American girl, Carter Mason, who looks after a princess (Demi Lovato) whose life is in danger. The film won the 2009 Teen Choice Award.

Selena gets into character with her co-star Andrew Seeley in the movie *Another Cinderella Story*.

Selena and Demi Lovato together again in the movie *Princess Protection Program*.

In 2009, she starred in a full-length *Wizards of Waverly Place* movie, and was the voice of Princess Selenia in two *Arthur* animated movies. But her big screen career really opened up in 2010, with *Ramona and Beezus*. It's about a little girl (Ramona) and her big sister (Beezus – played by Selena). Then, in 2011, Selena got two starring parts in the film *Monte Carlo* – a rich English girl, and her "double", Grace Bennett, from Texas.

"Monte Carlo was really fun ... It's basically a case of mistaken identity ... it's a romance, an adventure, a comedy ..."

At home

Although her life is very different from that of most teenagers, Selena has kept her feet on the ground. That's thanks largely to her mother, Mandy.

"I am around to make sure she doesn't change. ... She never goes to ... anything related to the business without a parent. That rule is not changing until she is 21!" Mandy Teefey. Selena's mother.

Selena at her 16th birthday party in Los Angeles, USA.

When she can, Selena likes, "sitting on the couch, watching movies, eating junk food, just relaxing with friends and family." Like any other teenager, she shares family chores which include feeding the dogs – Willie, Wallace, Fina, Chip and Chazz. Selena and her mother rescued Chazz in Puerto Rico while filming the *Wizards* movie.

Selena waits for her flight at Van Nuys Airport, California.

Friends are important. This is what Selena said about Demi Lovato: "You meet a lot of people that you may not be able to trust, so I'm happy that I have her."

Selena with singer, and close friend, Justin Bieber at the MTV Video Music Awards in 2011.

17

Selena and The Scene

Selena signed up with Hollywood Records (part of the Disney Music Group) in 2008. She'd already done some singing – including tracks from *Another Cinderella Story* and the theme song from *Wizards*, "Everything is Not What it Seems".

Selena with The Scene at the 2011 People's Choice Awards.

She joined up with a band, The Scene, and brought out three albums. *Kiss & Tell* (2009) rose to number nine in the US charts; *A Year Without Rain* (2010) got to number four and *When the Sun Goes Down* (2011) reached number three.

Selena during filming for the video to her song "Love You Like a Love Song".

"It gets overwhelming at times, the scheduling, with touring, acting ... Luckily, my mom is my manager, so I've always got her with me," she says. But being on stage gives her "an overwhelming sense of joy ... you see the crowds and you hear them ... it's the best!"

"Who Says", from *When the Sun Goes Down* – one of Selena's favourites, was awarded a **platinum certificate**, as was "Naturally" from *Kiss & Tell*.

Selena

fashion

As Alex Russo, and in real life, Selena's style used to be strictly casual. She once said her favourite shoes were Converse trainers.

Selena in a stunning purple silk mini-dress at the premiere of *Justin Bieber: Never Say Never.*

66 Fashion awareness is relatively new to me ... I've grown to love fashion through doing photo shoots recently ... Day-to-day I wear T-shirt and jeans ... on the red carpet I like to look elegant, and when I'm doing music, I go for more of an edgy look. 99

Now Selena has to dress up a lot more than she did. Her glitzy stage costumes and glamorous evening gowns have surprised some fans – they are used to seeing her as a kind of "girl next door"!

Selena shopping at French Connection in New York, USA.

In 2010 she started her own **fashion label**, Dream Out Loud. Selena said: "I wanted to make a line that was affordable and comfortable for my fans – stuff that I would wear, that you can dress up or dress down."

Selena's new clothing range at the launch in August 2011 at US chain store, Kmart.

21

Winning ways

When Selena looks back to *Barney*, she says, "It involved a lot of smiling ... Singing, dance routines — nothing that's going to help me win an Oscar one day."

Selena and actor Cory Monteith at the Kids' Choice Awards.

Selena has already won plenty of awards. As well as the 2009 Emmy for *Wizards*, she has also won:

* Young Artist for *Another Cinderella Story* (2009);
* Teen Choice for *Princess Protection Program* (2009) and for *Wizards* (2010);
* Kids' Choice (USA) as favourite TV actress in *Wizards* (2009, 2010 and 2011);
* ALMA for Comedy Actress in television (2009).

In 2011, Selena won Teen Choice for her songs "Who Says" and "Love You Like a Love Song". She also won People's Choice for a Favourite Breakout Artist.

Selena holds on to her ALMA Award in 2009.

One of her proudest moments was her high-school graduation, in 2010. It happened at the same time as her on-screen graduation in *Monte Carlo*.

Selena hosted the MTV Video Music Awards pre-show in 2011. "It's always been one of my favourite parts. It's a true honour," she said.

23

Taking on the world

In 2009, Selena became a UNICEF "goodwill ambassador". UNICEF is the world's leading organisation focusing on children and children's rights. The ambassadors help highlight their work.

Selena was only 17 when she became an ambassador – one of the youngest ever. Her first official mission was making a trip to Ghana.

Selena launches a UNICEF campaign in 2008.

"The trip was completely life-changing ... I feel very honoured to have a voice that kids listen to ... I feel very happy that I can use my voice to educate people ..."

Selena has also helped raise money for UNICEF in an annual "Trick or Treat" fund-raising drive at Halloween. In 2011 she made a trip to Chile, also working with UNICEF.

Selena has been involved with working for many other good causes, too – including raising money for helping stray dogs in Puerto Rico. (That's where she found her dog Chazz – see page 16.)

Fame and fans

Working on children's television for Disney made Selena a role model. Her time with Disney is over now, but she says, "That does not mean I want to completely disown the fact that I have a younger generation looking up at me ..."

Selena at the Teen Choice Awards in 2010.

She loves to keep in touch with her fans – but that has a downside. Some of them have been upset by her friendship with Justin Bieber – and they let her know! "I think the Internet can be … really evil. Something can instantly hurt your feelings," she says.

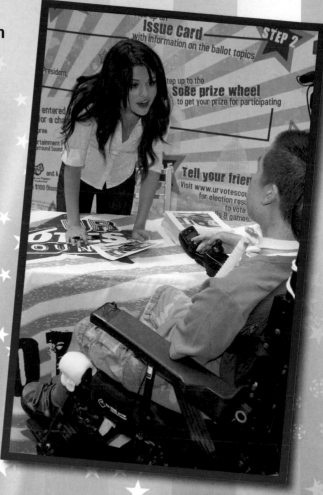

Selena at a teen event promoting awareness of national and world issues.

In 2011, Selena was rushed to hospital during a tour of the USA. She felt sick and dizzy. Luckily, her mum stepped in to make sure she took a break!

About fame, she says, "I've seen so many people who really let this business control their life. I don't want to let fame stop me from being myself."

A spellbinding future

> **"**I'd like to step out of comedy ... I'd love to do different genres. Anything that would challenge me as an actress.**"**

Selena is gradually creating a more grown-up image of herself. Her music is part of this. She says that it is now "a lot stronger" than it was.

Selena dances with Andrew Seeley in *Another Cinderella Story*.

She's often asked whether she wants to make singing or acting her long-term career. It looks as though she's most likely to settle for acting. She took her first steps in taking control of her own career in 2008, when she started her own production company, July Moon productions.

One more serious role she's playing is Hannah Baker, in a film version of a novel called "Thirteen Reasons Why", by Jay Asher. It's about a student who kills herself.

As for her private life, Selena says, "I feel that I should be able to grow up ... I've done the best I can."

Fan guide

Full Name: Selena Marie Gomez

Date of birth: 22 July 1992

Height: 1.68 metres

Hometown: Grand Prairie, Texas, USA

Record Label: Hollywood

Colour of eyes: Dark brown

Hobbies: Drawing, painting and cooking

There are many, many sites about Selena, and often they let you contribute to discussions about her. Remember, though, that it's OK to make comments, but it's not fair to be unkind. She cannot answer your comments herself!

http://selenagomez.com

http://selenagomezweb.com/
news/official-website/

http://selenadaily.org/

http://www.selena-fan.org/

http://www.allmusic.com/
artist/selena-gomez-p1063097/
biography

http://www.selenagomezfan.com

http://facebook.com/
SelenaGomez

http://twitter.com/selenagomez

http://youtube.com/selgomez

22 July 1992	Selena Marie Gomez is born
2002–2003	Plays Gianna in the series *Barney and Friends*
2006	Appears in *The Suite Life of Zack & Cody* as Gwen
2007–2008	Plays Mikayla in the series *Hannah Montana*
2007–2010	Plays Alex Russo in the series *Wizards of Waverly Place*
2008	Wins Nickelodeon Kids' Choice Award for *Wizards*
	Plays Mary Santiago in *Another Cinderella Story*
	Wins Young Artist Award for *Another Cinderella Story*
	Releases song "Tell Me Something I Don't Know"
	The voice of Helga in *Horton Hears a Who!*
2009	Plays Carter Mason in *Princess Protection Program*
	Plays Alex Russo in *Wizards of Waverly Place: The Movie*
	The voice of Princess Selenia in *Arthur and the Vengeance of Maltazard*
	The voice of Princess Selenia in *Arthur 3: The War of the Two Worlds*
	Releases songs "Naturally" and "Falling Down"
	Wins Teen Choice Awards for *Another Cinderella Story*, *Princess Protection Program*, and for *Red Carpet Icon*
	Wins Hollywood Style Award
	Wins ALMA Award – Special Achievement in Comedy
2010	Plays Beatrice "Beezus" Quimby in *Ramona and Beezus*
	Releases songs "A Year Without Rain" and "Round & Round"
	Wins Teen Choice Award for *Wizards*
	Wins Imagen Award for Best Young Actress in *Wizards*
2011	Plays Grace Bennett and Cordelia Winthrop Scott in *Monte Carlo*
	Releases songs "Who Says" and "Love You Like a Love Song"
2012	Plays Hannah Baker in *Thirteen Reasons Why*

Glossary

Cast The name for the group of actors performing in a play, film or TV show.

Fashion label A set of clothes designed by the person named on the label, or where a famous person uses their name to promote a certain style of clothing.

Gold record This is awarded to a singer or group after their album has sold at least 500,000 copies.

Platinum certificate An award for record sales of over 1 million copies.

Premiered First performed or shown on TV.

Producer The person who is responsible for the overall running of a show.

Role model Someone whom others look up to and want to be like.

Season A set of episodes of a particular TV series.

Index